Parachute Cord CRAFT

Quick & Simple
Instructions for
22 Cool Projects

Design Originals

an Imprint of Fox Chapel Publishing
www.d-originals.com

Contents

25

Josephine Knotted Necklace

27

Faux Wallet Chain

29

Crossed Square Knot Belt

31

Basic Lanyard

33

Adjustable Dog Collar & Lead

36

Camera Strap

38

Key Fobs

41

Button-Up Mug Wrap

43

Yoga Mat Harness

45

Decorative Flip-Flops

Introduction

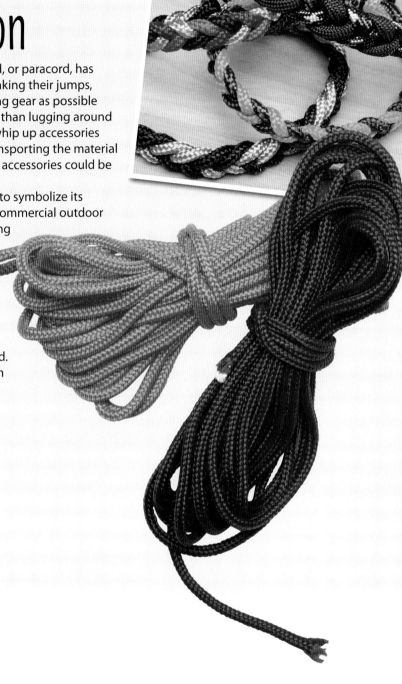

Originally used during World War II, parachute cord, or paracord, has since become a useful arts and crafts tool. After making their jumps, paratroopers would recycle as much of their landing gear as possible so they would be prepared for any setback. Rather than lugging around a large wad of cord from a chute, a soldier would whip up accessories such as belts, bracelets, and harnesses to make transporting the material convenient. If stuck in an emergency situation, the accessories could be taken apart to be reclaimed as roping.

Parachute cord became known as survival cord to symbolize its versatility, and became a popular product for the commercial outdoor market as a useful item to take on hiking or camping trips. Parachute cord can easily replace worn shoelaces on a pair of hiking boots or be used to strap camping gear together. As it became available in numerous fashion colors, parachute cord also began to appear in craft stores as a durable item to make accessories. The projects found in this book can be made using either 550 cord or the lighter weight 325 cord. The cord number refers to the military specification standards for the minimum tensile strength.

xt and illustrations by Samantha Grenier.

3N 978-1-57421-371-3

2012 by Pepperell Braiding Company and Design Originals, www.d-originals.com, an imprint of Fox Chapel Publishing, 800-457-9112, 1970 Broad Street, East Petersburg, PA 17520.

nted in China
cond printing

Tools

In addition to the cord itself, other accessories may be needed to complete a number of the projects in this book. To complete all the projects in this book, you will need a ruler, a pair of scissors, and a lighter for finishing. A paperclip will come in handy wherever noted if the cording will need to be woven back into the knots for finishing. A couple pairs of jewelry pliers may be necessary for jewelry projects that require the addition of chains, jump rings, or ribbon crimps.

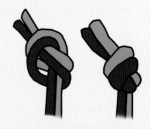

Knots to Know

Single Strand Overhand Knot

Double Strand Overhand Knot

Lark's Head Knot

Working with Chain

Links, chains, and jump rings may be necessary to help finish a project. Working with un-welded chains is easy. Opening and closing a chain link requires two pairs of pliers. Grasp the chain link you wish to open with both sets of pliers, positioning the pliers on opposite sides of the opening in the link (figure 1). Open the link by sliding one set of pliers away from you and the other toward you (figure 2). Opening the link this way helps the link keep its shape and keeps the seam tight. Don't pull the sides away from each other in opposite directions (figure 3). If you open the chain this way, when you go to close it, it will be difficult to match up the ends of the link again and achieve a tight seal. To close the link properly, use the same sliding motion that you did to open it.

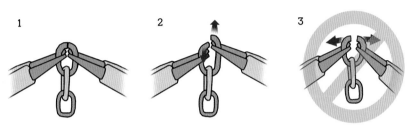

Ribbon Crimps

To finish a project without tying knots in the cord, you can use ribbon crimps to complete the project with chain and other findings. When working with parachute cord, you will need ribbon crimps at least ¾"–1" (2–2.5cm) wide (figure 1). Center the finished ends of your parachute cord between the teeth of the ribbon crimp (figure 2). Evenly pinch down on the crimp using a pair of pliers (figure 3).

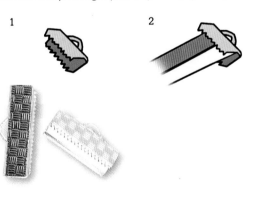

Cord Fusing 101

Melt all the cut ends of your parachute cord before beginning any project. This will make knot tying much easier because it prevents fraying. Melting and fusing require using the open flame of a lighter. A woodburning tool may be used for a controlled heat cut as well. It can take up to one minute for melted nylon to harden and cool, so **do not** touch the melted cord! Because melting and fusing involve working with a dangerous heat source, only a responsible adult should melt and fuse parachute cord.

When melting or fusing the cord, always hold the lighter vertically to prevent burns (figure 1). Melt only flush, clean ends; make a fresh cut with scissors if necessary (figure 2). Though the cord itself is made from 100 percent nylon, the colored shell and inner cord strands can melt at different rates. This can lead to uneven melting or even burning.

Fusing forms two strands of cord into one. You may need to do this for a project if you run short on material or would like to make a color change. To fuse your cord, hold the two ends of the separate strands parallel to one another, and trim the tips with scissors so that the ends are flush (figure 3). Hold the tips in the flame for about five seconds or until the melted cord begin to darken. Remove the flame and quickly force the two ends together (figure 4). With pressure, hold the ends together for about twenty seconds or until the melted points cool and harden.

WARNING
Using an open flame can cause burns and other injuries. Please use extreme caution when melting or fusing cords.

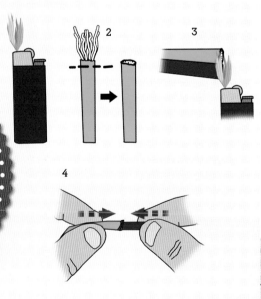

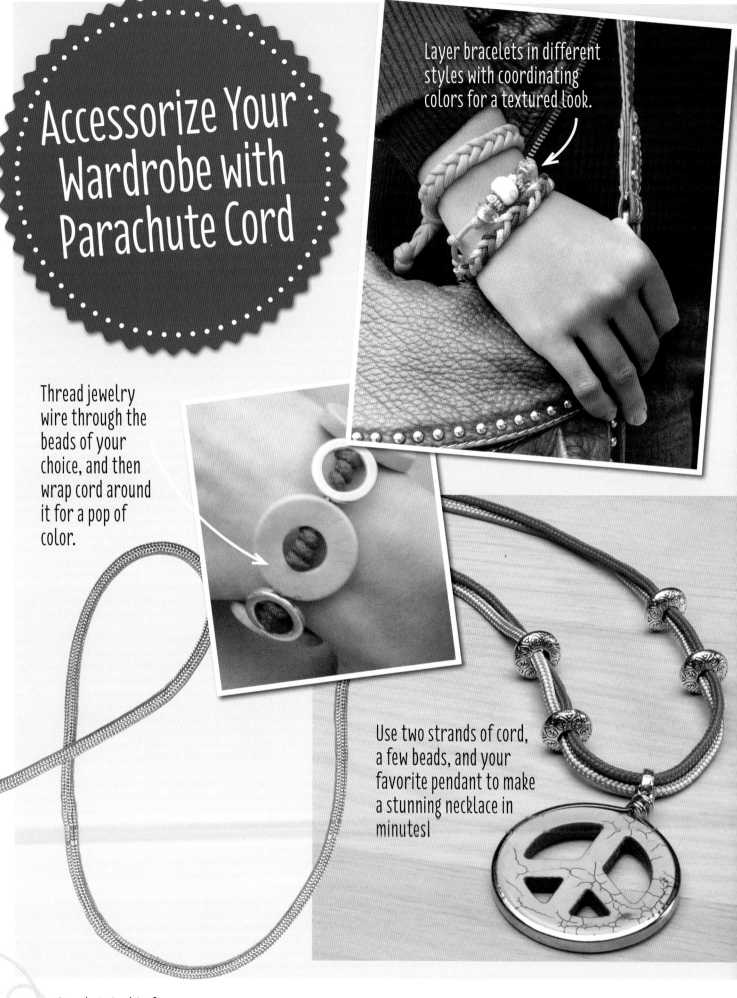

Accessorize Your Wardrobe with Parachute Cord

Layer bracelets in different styles with coordinating colors for a textured look.

Thread jewelry wire through the beads of your choice, and then wrap cord around it for a pop of color.

Use two strands of cord, a few beads, and your favorite pendant to make a stunning necklace in minutes!

A few basic accessories like a pendant or colorful bead can take your project to the next level!

Use jewelry wire to join two cord braids for a unique necklace.

Double the number of strands used to make the Simple Plaited Bracelet (page 10) for a thick cuff bracelet.

Keep it simple by using a single color.

Make the Simple Beaded Bracelet (page 12) with or without beads. It's up to you!

Simple Plaited Bracelet

A Colorful,
Customizable Accessory

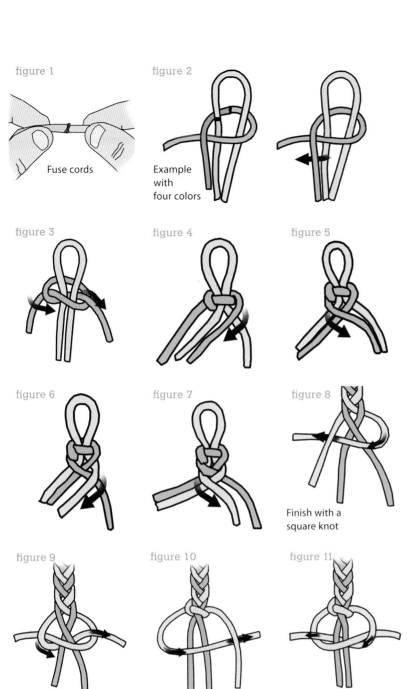

figure 1

Fuse cords

figure 2

Example
with
four colors

figure 3

figure 4

figure 5

figure 6

figure 7

figure 8

Finish with a
square knot

figure 9

figure 10

figure 11

figure 12

Tie off with an
overhand knot

Materials

- Two 3' (1m) lengths of 550 or 325 parachute cord for a two-color bracelet

- Four 18" (45cm) lengths of 550 or 325 parachute cord for a four-color bracelet

Step 1: When working with four different colors of parachute cord, fuse the ends of two strands together to form a 3' (1m) length of cord. Repeat with the remaining strands of parachute cord (figure 1).

Step 2: Find the center of both strands and position them as shown in figure 2.

Step 3: Form a half knot to attach the strands to one another (figure 3).

Step 4: Follow figures 4–7 to create a four-strand flat braid. Continue repeating the pattern until the bracelet reaches the desired length (about 6½"–7" [16.5–18cm] for most adults).

Step 5: Tie a square knot at the end of the bracelet to keep the braid from unraveling (figures 8–11).

Step 6: Using the center strands, tie a double strand overhand knot around the outer working strands to finish the end of the bracelet (figure 12). Make the knot small enough to pass through the loop on the opposite end of the bracelet, but not so small that it can slip back out after it is secured.

Simple Beaded Bracelet

A Touch of Flair

Materials

- One 24" (61cm) length of 325 parachute cord
- One 5' (1.5m) length of 325 parachute cord
- 4–6 large-hole beads

Step 1: Fold the 24" (61cm) length of cord in half and tie one bulky double strand overhand knot with the ends (figure 1). Turn and then center the 5' (1.5m) length of cord behind the 24" (61cm) length (figure 2).

Step 2: Follow figures 3–5 to form the simple weave.

Step 3: Feed the beads onto the cord and continue the weave (figures 6–8). Add one bead every other inch (2.5cm) or so.

Step 4: To finish, tie off with a square knot (figures 9–12). Tighten the knot. Trim away the excess cord and melt the ends to finish.

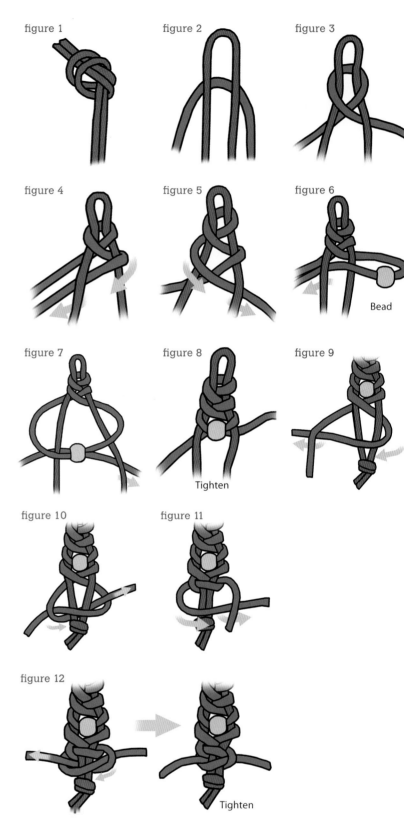

figure 1

figure 2

figure 3

figure 4

figure 5

figure 6

Bead

figure 7

figure 8

Tighten

figure 9

figure 10

figure 11

figure 12

Tighten

Chevron Chain Bracelet

Polished and Refined

Materials

- One 3' (1m) length of 325 parachute cord
- Three 6½"–7" (16.5–18cm) chains, one chain with an extra link
- One clasp closure
- One 2"–3" (5–7.5cm) length of extra chain or jump rings
- One board with pins

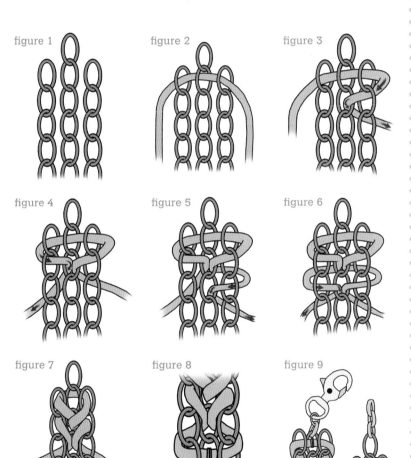

figure 1

figure 2

figure 3

figure 4

figure 5

figure 6

figure 7

Pull ends tight

figure 8

Fuse
ends together

figure 9

Step 1: Pin the lengths of chain to the board so that the links are parallel. Position the center length of chain so it is one link higher than the two outer chains (figure 1). Center the length of parachute cord in the first row of parallel links (figure 2).

Step 2: Pass the right strand of cord through the second link in the right chain and then through the corresponding link in the center chain. Bring the strand back out to the right side (figure 3).

Step 3: Following the same procedure, pass the left strand of cord through the second link in the left chain, and then through the corresponding link in the center chain. Bring this strand back out to the left side (figure 4).

Step 4: Following figures 5–7, continue weaving the cord through the chains until you reach the last row of links.

Step 5: To secure the cord, tie the ends together at the center, or trim and fuse the ends together as shown (figure 8).

Step 6: To finish the bracelet, add a clasp closure to the center link at one end and jump rings to the center link at the other end (figure 9).

Adjustable Bracelet

The Ultimate in Flexibility

figure 1

figure 2

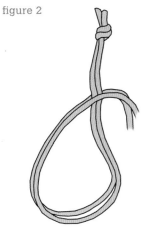

figure 3

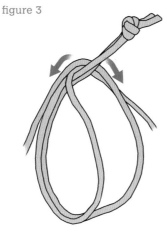

figure 4

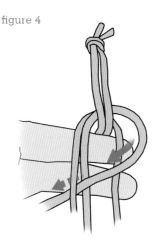

figure 5

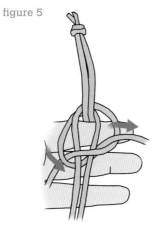

figure 6

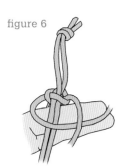

figure 7

figure 8

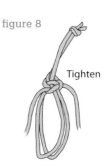

Tighten

Materials

- Two 4' (1m) lengths of 325 or 550 parachute cord

Step 1: Tie the ends of the parachute cord together using a double strand overhand knot (figure 1).

Step 2: Keeping the strands parallel, loop the cord toward itself, forming a shape similar to a lowercase d. The loop should be large enough to fit your wrist, with at least a 2" (5cm) tail so the bracelet can be adjusted (figure 2).

Step 3: Fold the strand ends around the tail, crossing them (figure 3).

Step 4: Form a square knot around the tail as shown in figures 4–8, making sure that first knot is good and tight.

Step 5: Repeat the square knot, working around the bracelet form until complete. Trim any excess cord from the bracelet and melt the ends to finish.

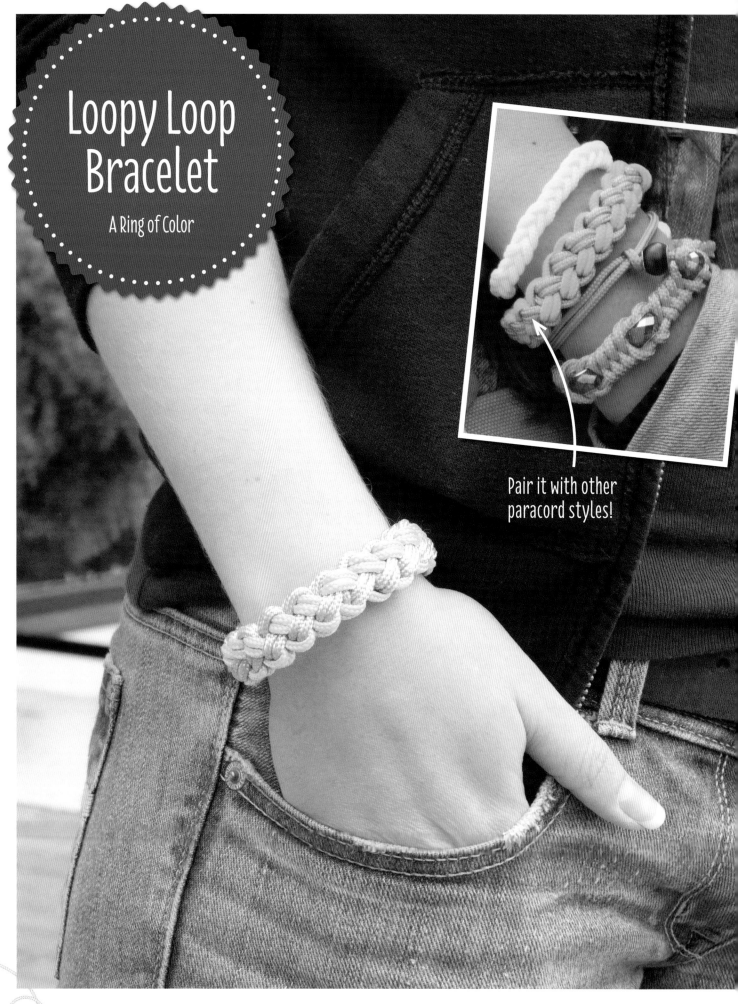

Loopy Loop Bracelet

A Ring of Color

Pair it with other paracord styles!

figure 1 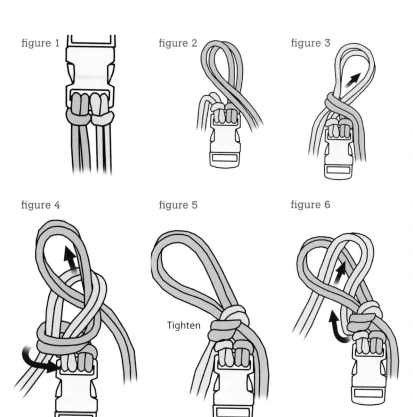 figure 2 figure 3

figure 4 figure 5 figure 6

Tighten

figure 7 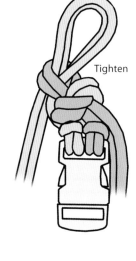 figure 8 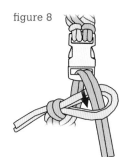 figure 9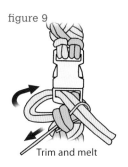

Tighten

Trim and melt

Materials

- Two 6' (2m) lengths of 325 parachute cord
- One 12mm plastic buckle
- One paperclip (for cord weaving)

Step 1: Center the two strands of parachute cord on one end of the plastic buckle, securing them with lark's head knots.

Step 2: Follow figures 2–7 to form a double loop weave.

Step 3: Repeat the double loop weave until the desired bracelet length is achieved.

Step 4: To close off the bracelet, run the free ends of the cord up through other end of the plastic buckle and through the final loop (figure 8). Tighten the loop. Pass the ends of the final loop cord through the plastic buckle and weave the ends into the bracelet using a paperclip (figure 9).

Step 5: Cut any excess cord from the bracelet and melt the ends to secure (figure 10).

Rosette Headband

Simple and Sweet

Try adding a
second rosette!

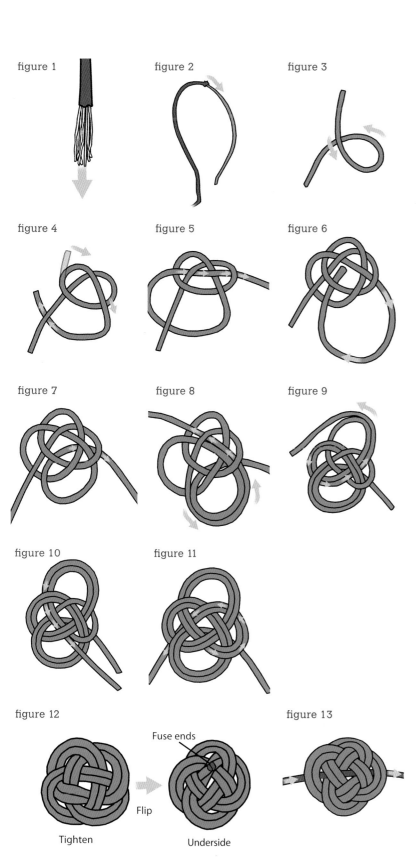

figure 1

figure 2

figure 3

figure 4

figure 5

figure 6

figure 7

figure 8

figure 9

figure 10

figure 11

figure 12

Tighten

Flip

Fuse ends

Underside

figure 13

figure 14

Materials
- One 18" (45cm) length of 550 parachute cord
- One 4' (1m) length of 550 parachute cord
- One ⅛" (5mm) thin metal headband (no teeth)

Step 1: Remove the white nylon filler from the center of the 18" (45cm) length of parachute cord (figure 1).

Step 2: Slide the cord over the headband to cover it (figure 2). Trim any excess and melt the ends in place.

Step 3: Form the rosette using the 4' (1m) length of cord by following the knot pattern in figures 3–7. Following figures 8–11, make a second pass through the knot with the other end of the cord. Keep the cords parallel; do not overlap the knots formed by the first end of the cord.

Step 4: Tighten the rosette knot as much as you can. This does take patience and often requires tightening one loop at a time. Once you have completed the knot, flip the rosette over. Trim and fuse the ends together on the underside of the rosette (figure 12).

Step 5: Slide the completed rosette onto the headband (figure 13), and guide it to the desired position (figure 14).

Simple Woven Headband
Keeping Every Strand in Place

Materials

- One 14" (35cm) length of 550 parachute cord
- One 16' (5m) length of 550 parachute cord
- One 1" (2.5cm) plastic headband
- Clear tape (optional)

Step 1: Remove the white nylon filler from the 14" (35cm) length of parachute cord. Melt the ends to prevent fraying (figure 1).

Step 2: Lay the 14" (35cm) length of parachute cord flat against the headband, positioning it in the center. Use a piece of tape to hold this piece in place until you create the first knot. Center the 16' (5m) length of parachute cord behind one end of the headband (figure 2).

Step 3: Follow figures 3–4 to complete the first half of a square knot. If desired, remove the tape used to secure the 14" (35cm) length of cord.

Step 4: Form the second half of the square knot, but this time fold the knot UNDER the center strip (figures 5–6).

Step 5: Following figures 7–10, continue forming square knots along the length of the headband, alternating creating the knots OVER and UNDER the center strip.

Step 6: Once you reach the other end of the headband, trim and melt the ends of any excess cord (figure 11).

figure 1

Melt ends

figure 2
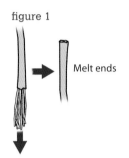

figure 3
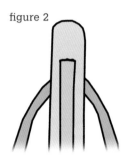

figure 4
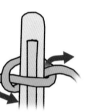

figure 5

Pass cord under strip

figure 6
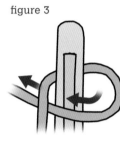
Tighten knot

figure 7

figure 8
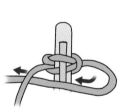
Tighten knot

figure 9
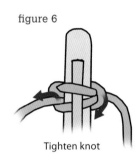
Pass cord under strip

figure 10

Tighten knot

figure 11
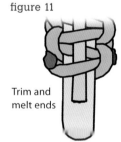
Trim and melt ends

Elegant Lengths Beaded Necklace

A Sophisticated Classic

Materials

- One 9' (3m) length of 325 parachute cord
- 6–10 large-hole beads

figure 1

Tighten loop

figure 2

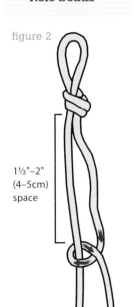

1½"–2" (4–5cm) space

figure 3

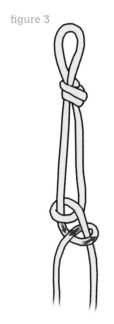

Step 1: Fold the length of cord in half and tie a double strand overhand knot at the center to form a loop (figure 1).

Step 2: About 1½"–2" (4–5cm) from the overhand knot, wrap the right strand around the left (figure 2), and then wrap the left strand around the right (figure 3). Tighten the knot, and slide a bead over both strands up to the knot (figure 4).

Step 3: Secure the bead in place by repeating the knot procedure (figures 5–7).

Step 4: Repeat figures 2–7 to continue forming the necklace. Tie off the end of the necklace with another double strand overhand knot (figure 8). Make the knot just small enough to pass through the loop formed at the opposite end.

figure 4

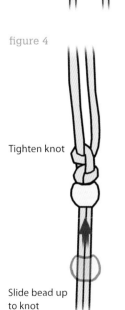

Tighten knot

Slide bead up to knot

figure 5

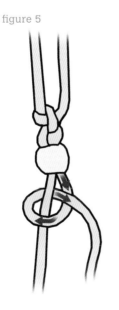

figure 6

figure 7

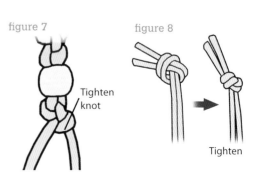

Tighten knot

figure 8

Tighten

Drop Chain Pendant Necklace

A Stunning Standout

Simplify this design by braiding the cord and using an overhand knot to attach the pendant

figure 1

figure 2

figure 3

figure 4

figure 5

Tighten loop

figure 6

figure 7

Tighten loop

figure 8

figure 9

Tighten loop

Trim and melt ends

figure 10

figure 11

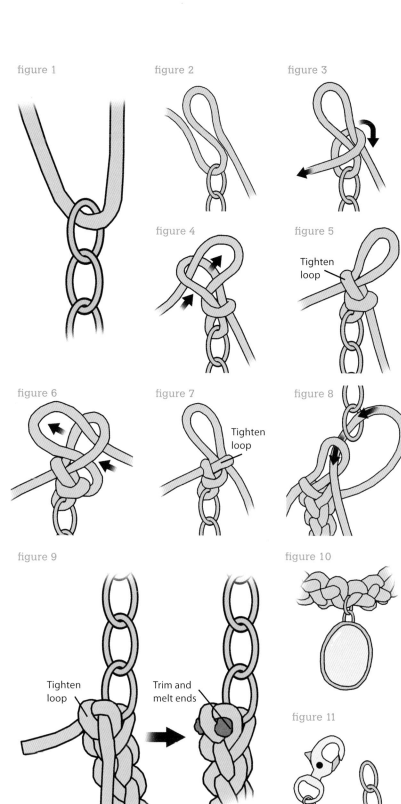

Materials

- One 6' (2m) length of 325 parachute cord

- Two 9"–10" (23–25cm) lengths of chain

- One clasp closure

- One pendant with a jump ring

Step 1: Center the length of cord on one end of the chain (figure 1).

Step 2: Follow figures 2–7 to form the loop weave.

Step 3: Repeat the loop weave pattern (figures 2–7) until only a small amount of cord remains. To complete the necklace, pass the free end of the cord through the end link of the remaining chain and down through the final loop in the cord (figure 8).

Step 4: Tighten the final loop. Trim away the excess cord and melt the ends to secure it in place (figure 9).

Step 5: Center the pendant on the length of woven parachute cord, and attach it using the jump ring (figure 10). Finish the necklace by attaching the clasp closure to one end of the chain (figure 11).

Double Woven Chain Necklace

Sturdy and Stylish

Materials

Makes an 18" (45cm)-long necklace.

- One 9' (3m) length of 325 parachute cord
- Two 3' (1m) lengths of large-hole jewelry chain (use two different styles of chain)
- One board with pins (optional)

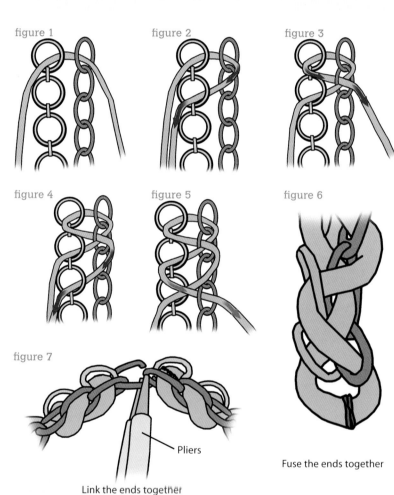

figure 1

figure 2

figure 3

figure 4

figure 5

figure 6

Fuse the ends together

figure 7

Pliers

Link the ends together

Step 1: Slide one end of the parachute cord through the end link of each of the chains, and center the strand between the chains (figure 1). Pin the chains in place if desired; this can be helpful as you work.

Step 2: Begin the zigzag weave by passing the right strand of parachute cord through the second link of the left chain (figure 2). Pass the left strand of parachute cord through the second link of the right chain (figure 3). The strands should crisscross, forming an X. Pull the cords tight.

Step 3: Repeat the zigzag weave, weaving the two lengths of cord through the chain links, continuing down the length of the necklace (figures 4–5). Sometimes, when using different styles of chain, the chain links may not line up perfectly. In this case, just skip the link that doesn't line up; this will not be noticeable when the necklace is completed.

Step 4: When you reach the ends of the chains, you can knot the ends of the cord together. For the cleanest finish, cut away any excess cord and fuse the ends together (figure 6).

Step 5: Complete the necklace by linking the ends of the chains together using an extra chain link or a jump ring (figure 7). The finished necklace should be long enough to slip over your head.

Josephine Knotted Necklace

A Full-Out Fashion Statement

Fashion-forward knotting

Materials

- Two 6' (2m) lengths of 550 parachute cord in color A
- Two 6' (2m) lengths of 550 parachute cord in color B
- Two ribbon crimps
- One clasp closure
- Several inches of extra chain or jump rings
- One board with pins

Step 1: Pair the cords of the same color together and work with them as one cord. Find the center of the cords in color A, and crisscross the cords to form a lowercase b shape (figure 1). Note: It may be helpful to pin this shape in place.

Step 2: Find the center of the cords in color B, and place the center point of the B cords over the loop formed by the A cords. Tuck the left strands of the B cords under the left tail of the A cords (figure 2).

Step 3: Follow figures 3–4 to form the Josephine knot. Tighten the knot by evenly tugging on all the cord ends (figure 5).

Step 4: Repeat the Josephine knot (figures 1–5) on either side of the first knot (figure 6). Repeat the Josephine knot four or five times as desired on either side of the initial knot before proceeding to the square knotting.

Step 5: Follow figures 7–11 to form a square knot. Continue making square knots, allowing about a 1" (2.5cm) gap between each knot.

Step 6: Repeat the square knots on both sides of the necklace until you have about 8"–10" (20–25cm) of square knots (figure 12).

Step 7: Trim the center strands on each end of the necklace evenly and melt the ends before pressing them into the ribbon crimps. The working strands forming the square knots can be trimmed flush with the last square knot on each end of the necklace and fused in place. Add the closure to one ribbon crimp and jump rings or chain to the other to finish the necklace (figure 13).

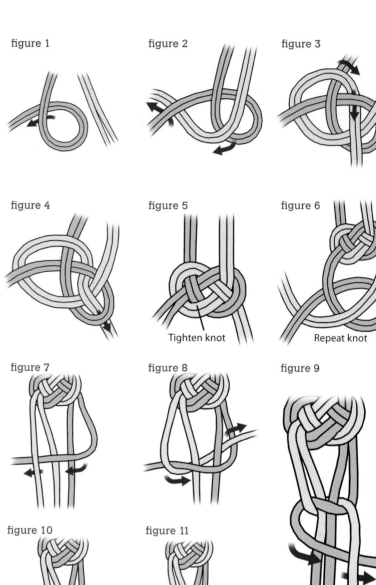

figure 1 figure 2 figure 3

figure 4 figure 5 figure 6

Tighten knot Repeat knot

figure 7 figure 8 figure 9

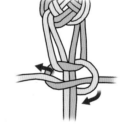
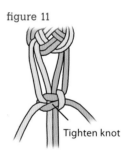
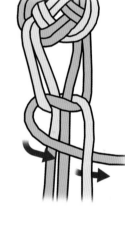

figure 10 figure 11

Tighten knot

figure 12 figure 13

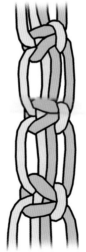
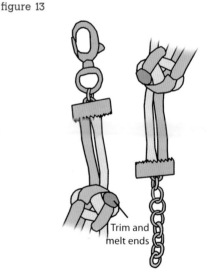

Repeat knot

Trim and melt ends

Faux Wallet Chain

Tough and Modern

Materials

- One 8' (2.5m) length of 550 parachute cord
- 1 large-hole bead
- 1 swivel spring hook or carabiner

Step 1: Fold the length of cord in half to find the center point. Creating about a 4" (10cm) loop, cross the right strand over the left (figure 1).

Step 2: Follow figures 2–5 to form a simple crown knot.

Step 3: Repeat figures 1–5 to form a line of simple crown knots. Leave a 1"–2" (2.5–5cm) gap between each knot to create the faux chain effect. Make 16"–18" (41–45cm) of faux chain.

Step 4: When you have completed the faux chain, loop both the ends of the cord through the end of the hook closure or carabiner (figure 6).

Step 5: Form a series of square knots by following figures 7–10. When very little cord remains, trim and melt the ends to secure it in place (figure 11).

Step 6: Slide a bead onto the loop at the opposite end of the chain (figure 12). Slide a wallet through the loop, positioning the loop at the fold of the wallet. Slide the bead tightly against the end of the wallet to secure it in place (figure 13). Clip the hook end of the chain to a belt loop on your pants and slip the wallet into your pocket.

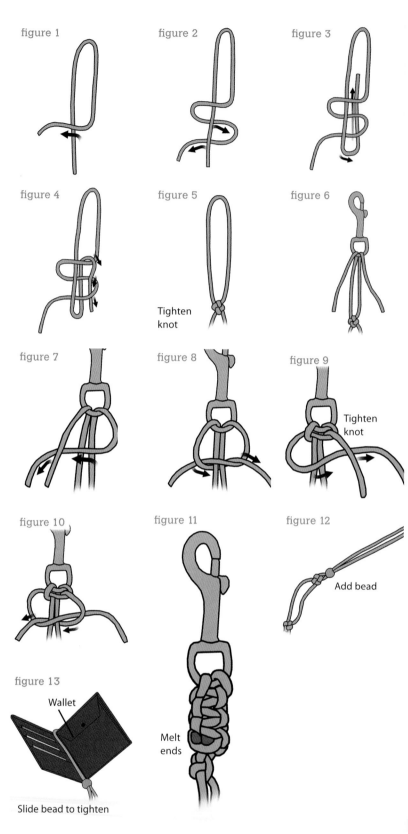

figure 1

figure 2

figure 3

figure 4

figure 5

Tighten knot

figure 6

figure 7

figure 8

figure 9

Tighten knot

figure 10

figure 11

Melt ends

figure 12

Add bead

figure 13

Wallet

Slide bead to tighten

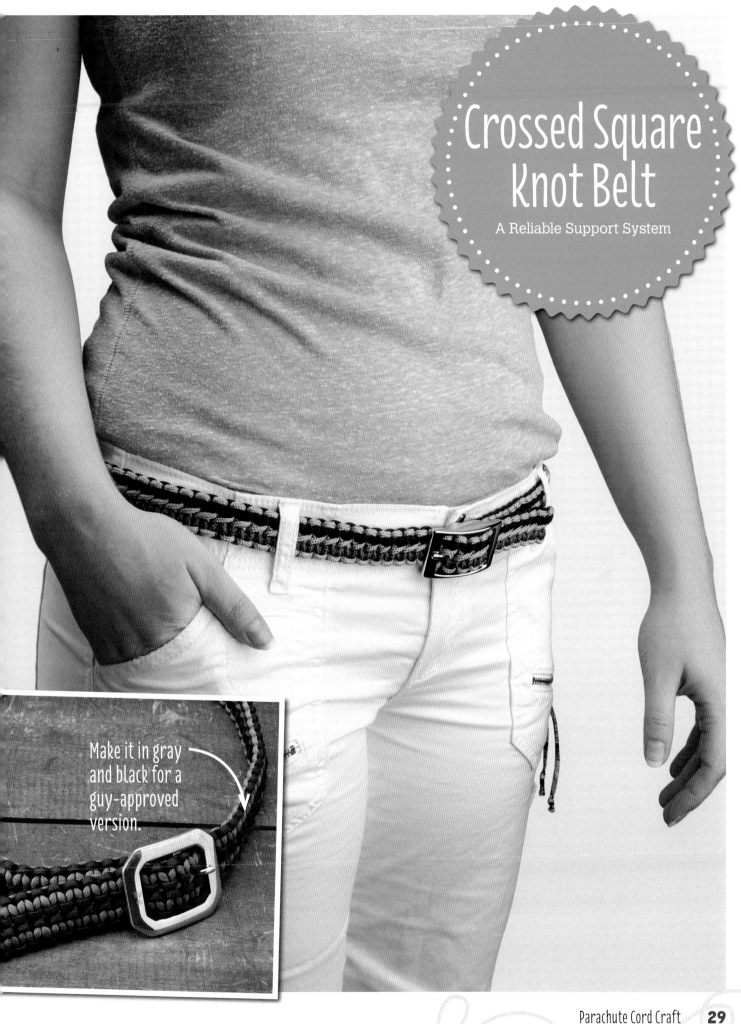

Crossed Square Knot Belt

A Reliable Support System

Make it in gray and black for a guy-approved version.

Materials

Note: The instructions for this project make one 40" (102cm) belt, which comfortably fits a 34" (86cm) waist. To make a larger belt, extra cord will be required.

- Two 16' (5m) segments of 550 parachute cord in color A
- Three 16' (5m) segments of 550 parachute cord in color B
- Two 16' (5m) segments of 550 parachute cord in color C
- One metal frame buckle

Step 1: Center the parachute cord (color B) around the pin of the metal frame buckle and secure using a lark's head knot. Secure colors A and C on either side (figure 1). Stagger the length of the inner strands from cords A and C. These strands should match the desired length for your belt. For example, for a 40" (102cm) belt, strands 2 and 5 should hang down 40" (102cm). This will be much shorter than the other working strands (figure 2).

Step 2: Beginning from the right, form a single square knot using strands 4 and 6. Follow figures 3–6 for instructions.

Step 3: Repeat the square knot procedure using strands 1 and 3, following figures 7–10.

Step 4: Before repeating the knotting process, crisscross the center strands (3 and 4) as shown, forming an X (figure 11). The strand from the left should always cross over the strand from the right.

Step 5: Repeat the knotting process by following figures 3–11 until the belt is complete. If you run out of cord on the outer working strands, fuse a new length of cord to each end using the method described on page 7 (this should not be necessary for the inner stationary strands).

Step 6: When the belt is complete, trim away any excess cord and melt the ends (figure 12).

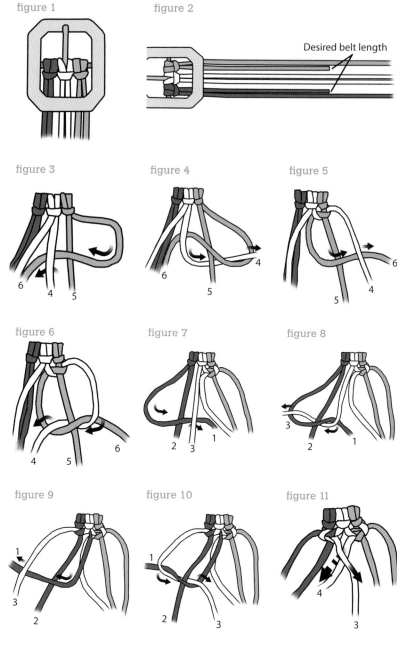

figure 1 figure 2 figure 3 figure 4 figure 5 figure 6 figure 7 figure 8 figure 9 figure 10 figure 11

Desired belt length

figure 12

Trim and melt

Basic Lanyard

A Campfire Classic

Materials

- Two 9' (3m) lengths of 325 parachute cord
- One key ring

Step 1: Center the two strands of parachute cord on the key ring. Adjust the cords so that like colors are parallel (figure 1).

Step 2: Follow figures 2–5 to form a round four-strand braid. Repeat until 12"–14" (31–35cm) of unbraided cord remains.

Step 3: Form the braided cord into a loop large enough to slip over your head. Shift strands 1 and 2 so that they are running behind the lanyard (figure 6).

Step 4: Treating the double strands as one, form a square knot around the braided cord (figures 7–12). Try shifting the center braid through the square knot to be sure this knot is not too tight.

Step 5: Form a second knot if possible by repeating figures 7–12. Trim any excess cord and melt the ends into the square knot.

figure 1
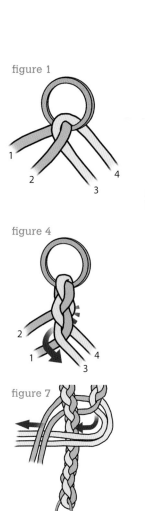

figure 2

Move the
back strand to front

figure 3

figure 4

figure 5

figure 6

figure 7
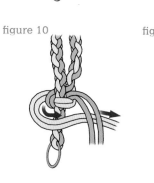

figure 8

figure 9

Keep knot a
little loose

figure 10

figure 11

figure 12

Tighten

Adjustable Dog Collar & Lead

A Functional Fashion Statement
for Man's Best Friend

Adjust the size
to fit any dog!

Collar Materials

Note: If the collar is being made for functional rather than decorative purposes, always use 550 parachute cord, especially for larger dog breeds.

- Two 10'–16' (3–5m) strands of 550 or 325 parachute cord (see sizing information at the right)
- Two 1½" (4cm) welded metal rings
- One 1" (2.5cm) welded metal ring
- Optional: One paperclip (or any other marker, such as a barrette)

Step 1: Measure your dog's neck and add 5"–6" (13–15cm) to this number. The result will be the final length of the dog collar.

Step 2: Set both strands onto one 1½" (4cm) metal ring using lark's head knots (figure 1). DO NOT position the strands so they have even lengths. Instead, stagger the cords so the center strands hang at the length of your dog collar. For example, if your final dog collar is going to be 24" (61cm) long, the center strands should hang down 24" (61cm). The outer strands will be much longer.

Step 3: Slide the outer strands through the second 1½" (4cm) ring. Set the ring close to the first set of lark's head knots (figure 2).

Step 4: Fasten the center strands together with a paperclip positioned 8"–10" (20–25cm) from the ends. This marks the location for the last ring.

Step 5: Follow figures 3–7 to form a square knot. Repeat the square knot until you reach the paperclip.

Step 6: Remove the paperclip and slide the 1" (2.5cm) ring onto the center strands as shown in figure 8.

Step 7: Following figures 9–13, continue forming square knots until the ends of the center strands are covered.

Step 8: Check the fit of the collar on your dog before finishing. When the collar is sized correctly, trim away any excess cord and melt the ends to prevent fraying and unraveling (figure 14).

figure 1

figure 2

figure 3

figure 4

figure 5

figure 6

figure 7

Tighten

figure 8

figure 9

figure 10

figure 11

figure 12

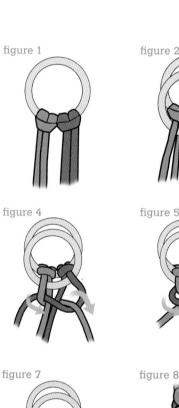
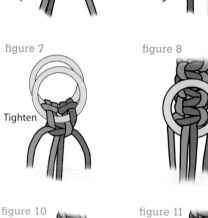
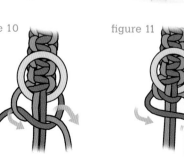
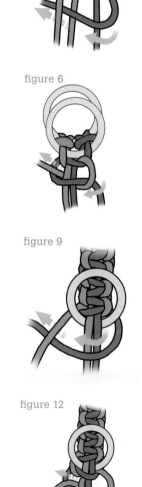

Sizing Information

- Small dogs: Use 9' (3m) of cord for a 12"–16" (31–41cm) collar (make the collar 20" [51cm] long)

- Medium dogs: Use 12' (4m) of cord for a 16"–18" (41–45cm) collar (make the collar 24" [61cm] long)

- Large dogs: Use 16' (5m) of cord for a 20"–24" (51–61cm) collar (make the collar 30" [76cm] long)

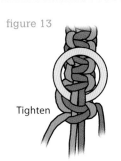

figure 13

Tighten

figure 14

Trim and melt

Lead Materials

- Two 16' (5m) strands of 550 parachute cord
- One metal leash hook or swivel spring hook
- One paperclip (for cord weaving)

Makes a 4'–5' (1–1.5m) leash.

Note: If the leash is going to be used regularly, use the 550 parachute cord for the strongest hold, and select a leash hook that can support your dog's weight.

Step 1: Center and attach the two lengths of parachute cord onto the metal leash hook using lark's head knots (figure 1).

Step 2: Follow figures 2–5 to form a round four-strand braid. Repeat the braid until 8"–10" (20–25cm) of loose cord remains.

Step 3: Fold the end of the leash down as shown in figure 6, forming a loop large enough for your hand. A 5"–6" (13–15cm) loop should be comfortable for most people.

Step 4: Using the paperclip, weave the loose parachute cord strands back into the leash. Follow the pattern formed by the braid (figure 7).

Step 5: When you run out of cord, or when the weave is 3" (7.5mm) long or more, trim away any excess and melt the ends in place (figure 8).

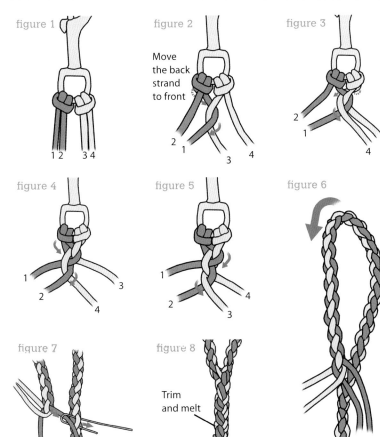

figure 1

1 2   3 4

figure 2

Move the back strand to front

2 1
3 4

figure 3

2
1
3
4

figure 4

1
2
3
4

figure 5

1
2
4
3

figure 6

figure 7

figure 8

Trim and melt

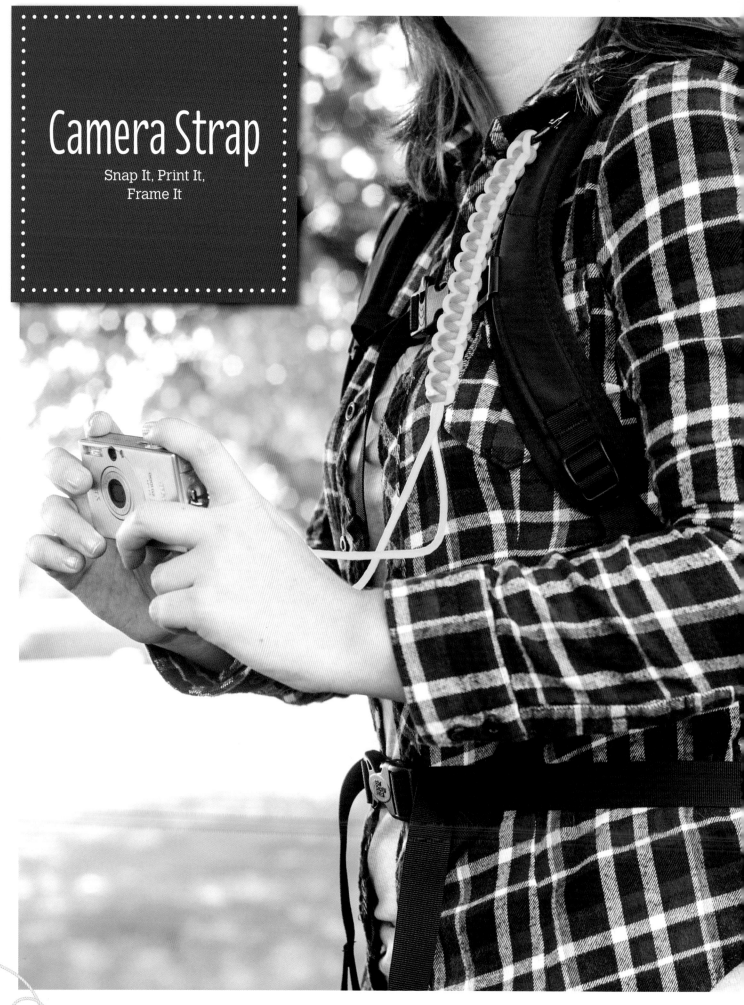

Camera Strap

Snap It, Print It,
Frame It

figure 1

Fuse cords

figure 2

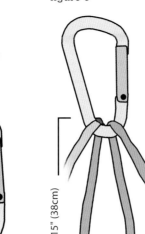

figure 3

15" (38cm)

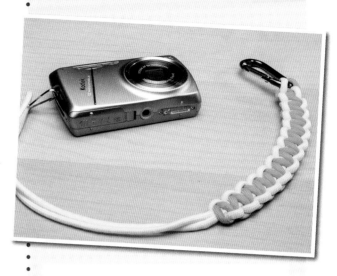

figure 4

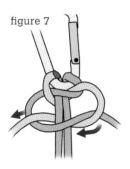

figure 5

figure 6

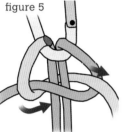
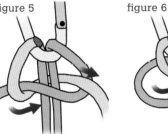

figure 7

figure 8

Materials

- One 6' (2m) strand of 550 parachute cord in color A

- One 6' (2m) strand of 550 parachute cord in color B

- One metal carabiner (or climber's hook)

- One lanyard snap

Step 1: Fuse the two strands of parachute cord together to form one 12' (4m) segment (figure 1).

Step 2: Fold a 15" (38cm) loop from the parachute cord, and pass the loop through the center of the carabiner. Center the cords on the hook so that the working strands are different colors (figures 2–3).

Step 3: Follow figures 4–7 to form a square knot. Repeat the knot until you run out of cord or until the knot pattern is about 6" (15cm) long.

Step 4: A lanyard snap can be secured to the end of the loop so the strap can be clipped to your camera (figure 8).

Key Fobs
Keeping What's Important Close

IF KEYS ARE FOUND, P
NEAREST AC
Property of Acme

figure 1

figure 2

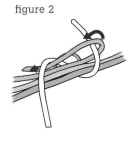

figure 3

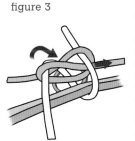

figure 4

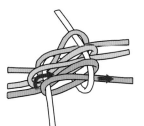

figure 5

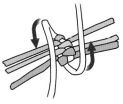

figure 6

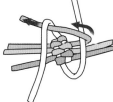

figure 7

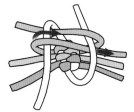

figure 8

figure 9

figure 10

figure 11

figure 12

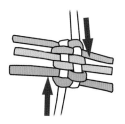

figure 13

figure 14

figure 15

Zigzag Key Fob

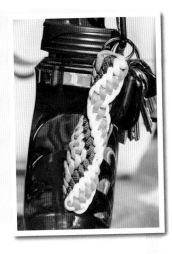

Materials

- Four 4' (1m) lengths of 550 parachute cord

- One metal key ring

- Optional: One board with pins (or tape)

Step 1: Center one strand of parachute cord on the metal key ring. This strand will act as a guideline.

Step 2: Lay the other strand segments across the guideline as shown in figure 1. Fold the ends of the guideline in opposite directions, forming loops. For a beginner, it may be easiest to tape or pin the guideline in place to prevent it from shifting.

Step 3: Follow figures 2–7 to form a square jumbo crown knot.

Step 4: Follow figures 8–14 to form a round jumbo crown knot. Repeat this knot for five layers.

Step 5: Form one square jumbo crown knot. This will change the direction of the twist (figure 15).

Step 6: Repeat steps 4 and 5 until the cord runs out.

Step 7: Trim any excess cord and melt the cord ends.

Square Stitch Set Up

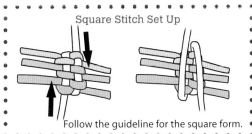

Follow the guideline for the square form.

Round Stitch Set Up

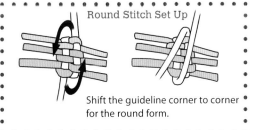

Shift the guideline corner to corner for the round form.

Chunky Round Crown Key Fob

figure 1

figure 2

figure 3

figure 4

figure 5

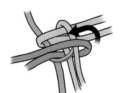 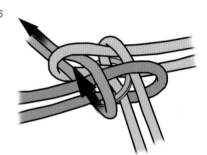

figure 6

figure 7

figure 8

Pull ends to tighten

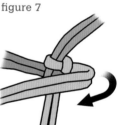

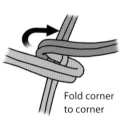

Fold corner to corner

figure 9

figure 10

Materials

- Four 3' (1m) lengths of 550 parachute cord
- One metal key ring

Step 1: Center and weave the cords around the metal key ring as shown in figure 1.

Step 2: Fold and weave the strands exactly as shown in figures 2–6. Be sure to fold the cords so that like colors are coming together. Tighten to secure the cords in place.

Step 3: Form a round crown knot by following figures 7–10, keeping like colors together.

Step 4: Repeat steps 7–10 until the key fob reaches the desired length or until you run out of cord. Trim any excess strands away and melt the ends in place.

Button-Up Mug Wrap

A Cozy Creature Comfort

Materials

Makes a wrap to fit a 3"–4" (7.5–10cm)-diameter thermos. For a larger wrap, add an extra foot (31cm) to each cut strand of parachute cord.

- Three 21' (6.5m) lengths of 325 parachute cord
- 3 large-hole buttons
- 1 board with pins
- Canteen, coffee mug, or thermos

figure 1

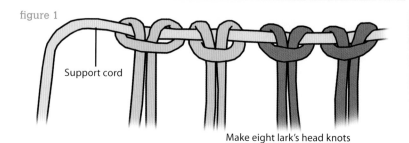

Support cord

Make eight lark's head knots

Step 1: Cut nine 6' (2m) lengths of the parachute cord. Center and pin one of the cords onto the board horizontally. This will be the support cord. Find the centers of the remaining eight strands and tie them onto the support cord using lark's head knots (figure 1). Note: For graphic purposes, only four lark's head knots are shown in figure 1.

Step 2: Follow figures 2–5 to form a square knot using the outer strands of two adjacent lark's head knots. Repeat the square knot across the row with each pair of lark's head knots (figure 6).

Step 3: On the next row follow figures 7–8 to create alternate square knots using the inner strands from the adjacent square knots formed previously. The square knots are tied exactly like they were in figures 2–5, but the pattern is shifted to the right by two strands.

Step 4: Form a small square knot at the end of the wrap using the support cord and strands from the end square knot as shown in figures 9–12. Repeat this knot at the other end of the wrap.

Step 5: Repeat figures 2–12 to form rows of square knots and alternate square knots until you have a 14" (35cm)-long rectangle. If possible, end on an alternate square knot row. Trim away any excess cord and melt the ends to secure the knots in place.

Step 6: Sew or knot the buttons onto one end of the finished wrap (figure 13). Align the buttons so that the size of the wrap can be adjusted. The wrap can be closed by sliding a button through one of the spaces created by the alternate square knot pattern.

figure 2

figure 3

figure 4

figure 5

figure 6

Form square knots across the whole row

figure 7

Form square knots on the alternate row

figure 8

figure 9

figure 10

figure 11

figure 12

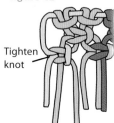

Tighten knot

figure 13

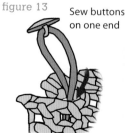

Sew buttons on one end

Yoga Mat Harness

Achieving Calm Serenity

Materials

Harness can be made to desired length; shown at 5' (2m) long.

- Three 16' (5m) segments of 550 parachute cord
- Two welded 1½" (4cm) metal rings
- One paperclip (for cord weaving)

figure 1   figure 2

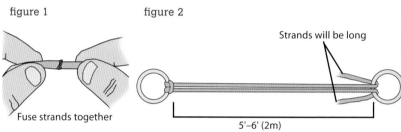

Fuse strands together   Strands will be long   5'–6' (2m)

figure 3   figure 4   figure 5

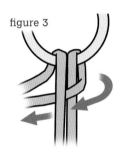      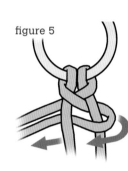

figure 6   figure 7   figure 8

   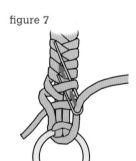   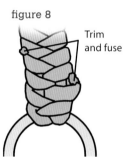

Trim and fuse

Step 1: Fuse the three 16' (5m) segments of parachute cord end-to-end to form one long 48' (15m) strand of cord (figure 1).

Step 2: Center the cord on one 1½" (4cm) ring, securing it with a lark's head knot. Pass the ends of the cord through the second metal ring. Space the rings 5'–6' (1.5–2m) from one another (figure 2).

Step 3: Follow figures 3–6 to form the weave, holding the center strands taut while forming the first few weaves. Repeat the weave up to the first ring. Keep the weave tight to prevent unraveling. The harness may want to twist as the weave is formed; this is normal. Just untwist the harness as you work to relax the cord.

Step 4: Finish by weaving the ends of the cord back into the harness. Use a paperclip to loosen the weave and pull the cord through (figure 7). Weave the ends back into the harness about 3"–4" (7.5–10cm) for a secure hold. Trim any excess cord and melt the ends if necessary. Tuck the melted cord tips into the harness (figure 8).

Step 5: To use the harness, push the strap through the metal rings and slide the rolled yoga mat through the loops (figure 9).

figure 9

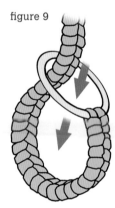

Decorative Flip-Flops
Durable Summer Footwear

Try different color combinations to suit your personal taste.

Materials

Instructions can be used for child or adult flip-flops.

- Two 16' (5m) lengths of 550 parachute cord (two 8' [2.5m] lengths for each shoe)
- Two 18" (45cm) segments of 550 parachute cord (one for each shoe)
- One pair of foam flip-flops

Step 1: Remove the strapping from the pair of foam flip-flops. Hang on to this to use as a template for the parachute cord straps.

Step 2: Center and crisscross two 8' (2.5m) strands of parachute cord (figure 1). Form a single square crown knot (figures 2–5) to make a stopper for the flip-flop. Pass the loose strands through the hole near the toe of one flip-flop. Insert the strands from bottom to top so the knot rests on the bottom of the flip-flop (figure 6).

Step 3: Follow and repeat figures 7 and 8 to form a round four-strand braid. Only about 2" (5cm) of braid will be necessary. This forms the portion of the strap that rests between your toes.

Step 4: Center and tie one 18" (45cm) segment of parachute cord to the two inner strands. Secure the segment with a single strand overhand knot (figures 9–10).

figure 1

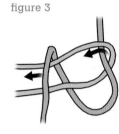

figure 2

figure 3

figure 4

figure 5

Pull ends to tighten

figure 6

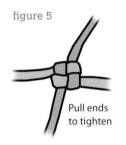
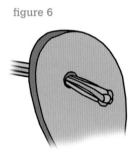

figure 7

figure 8

figure 9

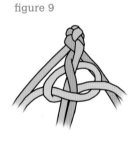

figure 10

figure 11

figure 12

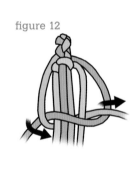

figure 13

figure 14

figure 15

figure 16

figure 17

figure 18

figure 19

figure 20

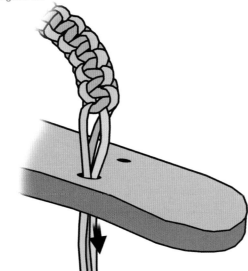

figure 21

Step 5: Follow figures 11–14 to form a square knot. Repeat to form a second square knot (figure 15). Divide the cords in half to form the straps.

Step 6: For the first strap, form a series of square knots using only three strands of cording. Use the shortest strand as the center strand (figures 16–19). Keep repeating the square knot until the desired strap length is achieved. The strap length may differ for each shoe size, so measure the length from your discarded flip-flop strap.

Step 7: Pass the strands through the corresponding strap hole in the flip-flop (figure 20).

Step 8: Turn the shoe to look at the bottom of the flip-flop. Follow figures 21–24 to form a three-strand knot. Repeat the knot if necessary. Cut off any excess cording and melt the ends. Careful with the lighter so that you don't burn the foam of the flip-flop!

Step 9: Repeat the instructions from steps 6-8 to form the second strap of the flip-flop.

Step 10: Repeat steps 2–9 to complete the second shoe.

figure 22

figure 23

figure 24

More Great Books from Design Originals

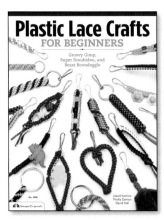

Plastic Lace Crafts for Beginners
ISBN 978-1-57421-367-6 **$8.99**
DO3490

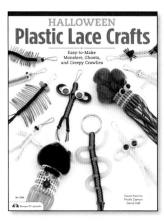

Halloween Plastic Lace Crafts
ISBN 978-1-57421-383-6 **$8.99**
DO3506

Awesome Foam Craft
ISBN 978-1-57421-352-2 **$9.99**
DO3475

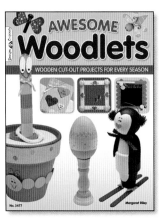

Awesome Woodlets
ISBN 978-1-57421-354-6 **$8.99**
DO3477

Crafty Parties for Kids
ISBN 978-1-57421-353-9 **$9.99**
DO3476

**Making Jewelry with
T-Shirt Yarn**
ISBN 978-1-57421-374-4 **$8.99**
DO3498

Felt from the Heart
ISBN 978-1-57421-365-2 **$9.99**
DO3488

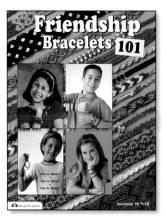

Friendship Bracelets 101
ISBN 978-1-57421-212-9 **$7.99**
DO3335

Friendship Bracelets 102
ISBN 978-1-57421-294-5 **$8.99**
DO3442